Sahil Sholla

Performance Evaluation of Clustering Algorithms in Wireless Sensor Networks (WSN). Energy Efficiency of S-Web and LEACH

GRIN Publishing

Bibliographic information published by the German National Library:

The German National Library lists this publication in the National Bibliography; detailed bibliographic data are available on the Internet at http://dnb.dnb.de .

Imprint:

Copyright © 2013 GRIN Verlag GmbH
Print and binding: Books on Demand GmbH, Norderstedt Germany
ISBN: 978-3-656-93001-3

This book at GRIN:

http://www.grin.com/en/e-book/293888/performance-evaluation-of-clustering-algorithms-in-wireless-sensor-networks

GRIN - Your knowledge has value

Since its foundation in 1998, GRIN has specialized in publishing academic texts by students, college teachers and other academics as e-book and printed book. The website www.grin.com is an ideal platform for presenting term papers, final papers, scientific essays, dissertations and specialist books.

Visit us on the internet:

http://www.grin.com/

http://www.facebook.com/grincom

http://www.twitter.com/grin_com

Performance Evaluation of
Clustering Algorithms in WSN

Thesis submitted to the department of

Electronics and Communication Engineering

of

National Institute of Technology Srinagar

in partial fulfillment of the requirements

for the degree of

Master of Technology

by

Sahil Sholla

Department of Electronics and Communication Engineering

National Institute of Technology Srinagar

J&K, India

July 2013

Abstract

Wireless Sensor Networks (WSNs) are highly integrated technologies applying sensors, microcontrollers and wireless networks technologies. Wireless sensor networks (WSNs) is a promising technology that has a large spectrum of applications such as, battlefield reconnaissance, border protection and security surveillance, preparing forecasts, severe environment detection, volcano monitoring, disaster management. WSNs operate unattended in harsh environments with limited energy supplies that can't be practically changed or recharged. Thus energy efficiency is a critical design issue which must be addressed.

Clustering plays an effective role in judicious use of dwindling energy resources of the deployed sensor nodes. Nodes are grouped into clusters and a specific designated node, called the cluster head is responsible for collecting data from the nodes in its cluster, aggregating them and sending to the BS, where data can be retrieved later. Besides energy efficiency, clustering has many other advantages like reduced routing overhead, conservation of communication bandwidth, stabilized network topology, network stability etc.

In this research, we study the energy efficiency of two clustering algorithms, S-Web and LEACH and compare them for network lifetime. Simulation results show that the S-Web clustering mechanism achieves a noticeable improvement in the network lifetime.

Keywords:

Clustering, Energy Efficiency, SWEB, Wireless Sensor Networks, LEACH, Network Lifetime

1

Acknowledgement

I am heartily grateful to my supervisor, *Mr. Ghulam Rasool Begh*, whose patient encouragement, guidance and insightful criticism from the time to time helped me to establish the overall direction of the research.

I also express profound gratitude to my parents who stood by me through thick and thin and all the friends whose valuable suggestions and support helped me during the completion of my thesis.

Sahil Sholla

Contents

Glossary

Glossary Term	Description
Base station (BS)	An information processing center where all data that have been sensed by the sensor nodes are collected, processed and stored for later retrieval.
Cluster	It is a group of nodes in a network that are grouped together to reduce energy consumption during data transmission.
Cluster Head (CH)	It is a node responsible for collecting data from other nodes, aggregates them and sends them to the base station where they can be retrieved later.
MANET	Mobile Ad hoc Network
WSNs	Wireless Sensor Networks
Homogeneous	It means that sensor nodes are having uniform structure and of the same or similar nature.
Inter-Cluster communication	Data reception and transmission between clusters.
Intra-Cluster communication	Data reception and transmission within one cluster.
Network Lifetime	The lifetime of a network is the active time of the network until the first node runs out of energy.
Wireless Sensor Network	Large number of micro-sensors that communicate wirelessly and bring themselves together to form a network.
S-Web	Sensor Web
LEACH	Low Energy Adaptive Clustering Hierarchy

CHAPTER 1

INTRODUCTION

Recent advances in high integration technologies and low power design have brought to the fore small-sized battery- operated sensors that are capable of monitoring the environment. A typical node of a WSN is equipped with four components: a sensor that performs the sensing of required events in a specific field, a radio transceiver that performs radio transmission and reception, a microcontroller: which is used for data processing and a battery that is a power unit providing energy for operation [1]. These sensor nodes can be deployed randomly to perform such applications as monitoring environment, battlefield reconnaissance, border protection and security surveillance, preparing forecasts, volcano monitoring etc. In disaster management situations such as earthquakes, volcanic eruptions, tornadoes etc sensor networks can be used to locate the affected regions and direct emergency relief to the survivors. In military situations (Fig. 1), sensor networks can be used in surveillance missions and can be used to detect moving targets, chemical gases, or the presence of micro-agents [2].

The hallmark of wireless sensors networks (WSNs) is their ability to function unattended in harsh environments in which contemporary human-in-the-loop monitoring schemes are unproductive, precarious, and infeasible. Therefore, sensors are likely to be deployed arbitrarily in the area of concern by fairly hysterical means, e.g. dropped by a helicopter, and to collectively form a network in an ad-hoc manner.

However, the limited energy of each node, supplied from non-rechargeable batteries, with no form of recharging after deployment and the possibility of having damaged nodes during deployment is one of the most crucial problems in WSN. Given the important of energy efficiency in WSNs, most of the algorithms proposed for WSNs concentrate mainly on maximizing the lifetime of the network by trying to minimize the energy consumption. Other application specific design objectives like high fidelity target detection and classification, security, real time communication etc may also considered.

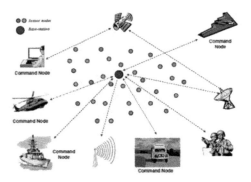

Clustering is proven to be an effective approach to conserve limited energy resources, provide better data aggregation and scalability of WSNs [3].Clustering is defined as the grouping of similar objects or the process of finding a natural association among some specific objects or data [4]. In WSN it is used to minimize the number of nodes that take part in long distance data transmission to a BS, what leads to lowering of total energy consumption of the system. Clustering reduces the amount of transmitted data by grouping nearby nodes and electing a specific node as a cluster head, where aggregation of data is performed to avoid redundancy and communication load caused by multiple transmissions, then the aggregated data is sent to the next cluster head or to the BS, where it is processed, stored or retrieved.

This thesis analyses the energy efficiency of S-Web and LEACH clustering algorithms to understand how it influences the network lifetime. The thesis is divided into five chapters, Chapter One presents an introduction to the WSN, Chapter Two provides literature survey on clustering WSN, Chapter Three presents problem definition and implementation, Chapter four discusses the results of the simulation and Chapter Five concludes the research and also defines possible future enhancements.

CHAPTER 2

LITERATURE SURVEY

2.1 Clustering ad hoc networks

Ad hoc network is a self-organizing multihop system of wireless nodes which can communicate with each other without pre-existing infrastructure. In an ad hoc network, mobile nodes communicate with each other using multihop wireless links. There is no stationary infrastructure; for instance, there are no base stations. Each node in the network also acts as a router, forwarding data packets for other nodes. The development of dynamic routing protocols that can efficiently find routes between two communicating nodes is a crucial research issue in the design of ad hoc networks [5]. The routing protocol must be able to keep up with the high degree of node mobility that often changes the network topology. The routing protocols in ad hoc networks are different compared to normal wired networks. The use of conventional routing protocols in a dynamic network is inconvenient because they place a heavy computational burden on mobile computers and they present convergence characteristics that don't suit well enough the needs of dynamic networks [6]. For instance, any routing scheme in a dynamic environment such as ad hoc networks must consider that the topology of the network can vary while the packet is being routed [6] and that the quality of wireless links is highly variable. In wired networks, link failure is not frequent since the network structure is mostly static. Therefore, routes in MANET must be calculated much more frequently in order to keep up the same response level of wired networks [8].

Moreover, the limited energy of each node, supplied from non-rechargeable batteries, with no form of recharging after deployment and the possibility of having damaged nodes during deployment is one of the most crucial problems in WSN. Many routing protocols have been proposed for WSNs. Most of the algorithms proposed for WSNs concentrate mainly on maximizing the lifetime of the network by trying to minimize the energy consumption.

Researchers agree that a successful method for dealing with the maintenance problem of mobile ad hoc networks and lifetime for wireless sensor networks is clustering [3]. With an ad hoc clustering network, the nodes are separated into groups called clusters. There are usually three types of nodes in clustering networks, as shown in Figure 2: cluster heads (CHs), gateway nodes and normal nodes. In each cluster, one node is elected as a CH to act as a local controller. The size of the cluster (the number of nodes in the cluster) depends on the transmission range of the nodes in single hop cluster and the number of hops made by the cluster in multi-hop clusters. The normal node sends or relays data to the CH which transfers the collected packets to the next hop. The gateway node, belonging to more than one cluster, bridges the CHs in those clusters. Both CHs and gateway nodes form the backbone network, yet the presence of gateway node is not compulsory in the clustering network [9].

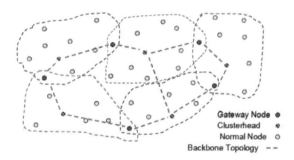

Figure 2 Clustering Network

Moreover, base station (BS) provides the communication link between the sensor network and the end-user. It is normally the sink in a WSN. The data in a sensor network can be used for a wide-range of applications. Data are generated in WSNs in response to queries received from the end user.

In clustering ad hoc networks, both proactive and reactive routing protocols are used. Connectivity within a cluster, only containing a small number of nodes, is maintained by periodically exchanging information updates among neighboring nodes about links changes. Therefore, when a node sends data to its CH, a route-table based routing (proactive) protocol is used. However, if the destination node is in a different cluster, the CH that the node belongs to will need to discover the backbone route so that the inter-cluster routing is on-demand (reactive).

Clustering schemes can be classified into ad hoc sensor network clustering schemes and mobile ad hoc network clustering schemes. In sensor networks, the energy stored in the network nodes is limited and usually infeasible to recharge; the clustering schemes for these networks therefore aim at maximizing the energy efficiency. In mobile ad hoc networks, the movement of the network nodes may quickly change the topology resulting in the increase of the overhead message in topology maintenance; the clustering schemes for mobile ad hoc networks therefore aim at handling topology maintenance, managing node movement or reducing overhead[9].

2.2 Advantages of Clustering

Grouping sensor nodes into clusters has been widely pursued by the research community in order to achieve the network scalability objective [2]. Clustering offers numerous advantages, in addition to supporting network scalability; it can localize the route set up within the cluster and thus reduce the size of the routing table stored at the individual node [10]. Clustering can also conserve communication bandwidth since it limits the scope of inter-cluster interactions to CHs and avoids redundant exchange of messages among sensor nodes [11]. Moreover, clustering can stabilize the network topology at the level of sensors and thus cuts on topology maintenance overhead. Sensors would care only for connecting with their CHs and would not be affected by changes at the level of inter-CH tier [12].Only the CHs and gateway nodes form the backbone network, resulting in much simpler topology, less overhead, flooding and collision. [9]. The CH can also implement optimized management strategies to further enhance the network operation and prolong the battery life of the individual sensors and the network lifetime [11]. A CH can schedule activities in the cluster so that nodes can switch to the low-power sleep mode most of the time and reduce the rate of energy consumption. Sensors can be engaged in a round-robin order and the time for their transmission and reception can be determined so that the sensors reties are avoided, redundancy in coverage can be limited and medium access collision is prevented [13-16]. Furthermore, a CH can aggregate the data collected by the sensors in its cluster and thus decrease the number of relayed packets [17].

2.3 Challenges for Clustering Algorithms

Clustering schemes play an important role in WSN; these can effectively improve the network performance. There are several key limitations in WSNs that clustering schemes must consider.

• **Limited Energy:** Wireless sensor nodes are small size battery operated sensors, so they have limited energy storage. It is not practicable to recharge or replace their batteries after exhaustion. The clustering algorithms are more energy efficient compared to the direct routing algorithms [3]. This can be achieved by balancing the energy consumption in sensor nodes by optimizing the cluster formation, periodically re-electing CHs based on their residual energy, and efficient intra-cluster and inter-cluster communication.

• **Maximal network longevity:** Since sensor nodes are energy-constrained, the network's lifetime is a major concern; especially for applications of WSNs in harsh environments. When CHs are richer in resources than sensors, it is imperative to minimize the energy for intra-cluster communication. If possible, CHs should be placed close to most of the sensors in its clusters [2]. On the other hand, when CHs are regular sensors, their lifetime can be extended by limiting their load. Combined clustering and route setup has also been considered for maximizing network's lifetime [18] . Adaptive clustering is also a viable choice for achieving network longevity.

• **Constrained resources:** The small physical size and small amount of stored energy in a sensor node limits many of the abilities of nodes in terms of processing, memory, storage, and communication.

• **Secure Communication:** The ability of a WSN to provide secure communication is ever more important when considering these networks for military applications [19]. The self-organization of a network has a huge dependence on the application it is required for. An establishment of secure and energy efficient intra-cluster and inter-cluster communication is one of the important challenges in designing clustering algorithms since these tiny nodes when deployed are unattended to in most cases.

• **Cluster formation and CH selection:** Cluster formation and CHs selection are two of the important operations in clustering algorithms. Energy wastage in sensors in WSN due to direct transmission between sensors and a base station can be avoided by clustering the WSN. Clustering further enhances scalability of WSN in real world applications. Selecting optimum cluster size, election and re-election of CHs, and cluster maintenance are the main issues to be addressed in designing of clustering algorithms [3]. The selection criteria to isolate clusters and to choose the CHs should maximize energy utilization.

• **Load balancing:** Even distribution of sensors among the clusters is usually an objective for setups where CHs perform data processing or significant intra-cluster management duties [20]. Given the duties of CHs, it is intuitive to balance the load among them so that they can meet the expected performance goals [21]. Load balancing is a more pressing issue in WSNs where CHs are picked from the available sensors. In such case, setting equal-sized clusters becomes crucial for extending the network lifetime since it prevents the exhaustion of the energy of a subset of CHs at high rate and prematurely making them dysfunctional [2]. Even distribution of sensors can also leverage data delay. When CHs perform data aggregation, it is imperative to have similar number of node in the clusters so that the combined data report becomes ready almost at the same time for further processing at the base-station or at the next tier in the network.

• **Minimal cluster count:** This objective is particularly common when CHs are specialized resource-rich nodes [22]. The network designer often likes to employ the least number of these nodes since they tend to be more expensive and vulnerable than sensors. For example, if CHs are laptop computers, robots or a mobile vehicle there will be inherently some limitation on the number of nodes. The limitation can be due to the complexity of deploying these types of nodes, e.g. when the WSN is to operate in a combat zone or a forest [2]. In addition, the size of these nodes tends to be significantly larger than sensors, which makes them easily detectable. Node visibility is highly undesirable in many WSNs applications such as border protection, military reconnaissance and infrastructure security.

• **Synchronization:** When considering a clustering scheme, synchronization and scheduling will have a considerable effect on the overall network performance. Slotted transmission schemes such as TDMA allow nodes to regularly schedule sleep intervals to minimize energy used. Such schemes require synchronization mechanisms to setup and maintain the transmission schedule.

• **Data Aggregation:** Data aggregation eradicates duplication of data. In a large network there are often multiple nodes sensing similar information. Data aggregation allows differentiation between sensed data and useful data. Many clustering schemes providing data aggregation capabilities [23] must carefully select a suitable clustering approach.

• **Fault-tolerance:** In many applications, WSNs will be operational in harsh environments and thus nodes are usually exposed to increased risk of malfunction and physical damage. Tolerating the failure of CHs is usually necessary in such applications in order to avoid the loss of important sensors' data. The most intuitive way to recover from a CH failure is to re-cluster the network. However, re-clustering is not only a resource burden on the nodes, it is often very disruptive to the on-going operation [2]. Therefore, contemporary fault-tolerance techniques would be more appropriate for that sake. Assigning backup CHs is the most notable scheme pursued in the literature for recovery from a CH failure. The selection of a backup and the role such spare CH will play during normal network operation varies. When CHs have long radio range, neighboring CHs can adapt the sensors in the failing cluster [24]. Rotating the role of CHs among nodes in the cluster can also be a means for fault-tolerance in addition to their load balancing advantage [25].

• **Quality of Service (QoS):** From an overall network standpoint, we can look at QoS requirements in WSNs. Many of these requirements are application dependant such as acceptable delay and packet loss tolerance. Existing clustering algorithms for WSN mainly focus on providing energy efficient network utilization, but pay less attention to QoS support in WSN. QoS metrics must be taken into account in the design process [3].

2.4 Clustering Schemes for Sensor Networks

The limited energy of sensor nodes supplied from non-rechargeable batteries is undoubtedly one of the most crucial problems in WSN. With the evolving trend in application and management of

13

WSN, clustering provides an efficient means of managing sensor nodes in order to prolong its lifetime. Several clustering techniques for WSN have been developed to extend the lifetime of sensor networks.

2.4.1 Optimizing Cluster Organization

Cluster organization details how to partition clusters and to select CHs, how to define cluster size and how to assign transmission ranges to the nodes, all of which will affect the power consumption of the network. Therefore, optimizing the cluster organization can improve energy efficiency.

2.4.1.1 Minimizing total distances to CH

This method optimizes the organization of the clusters and the selection of the CHs to achieve the minimum sum of the square of distance between the normal nodes and their CHs. The energy e to transmit a message from a source to a receiver depends on the distance d between them: $e = k \, d^c$, $(2<c<4)$, (1) where k and c are constants for a specific wireless system, and where usually $2<c<4$. These distances are affected by how the nodes are organized into clusters. *S. Ghiasi et* al. [26] propose an optimal algorithm for clustering the sensor nodes so that the sum of the square of distance of the normal nodes from their CHs is minimized

2.4.1.2 Assigning the lowest transmission power needed

The method optimizes the cluster organization by assigning to the normal nodes, or the CHs the lowest power needed for intra-cluster communication, and also the gateway nodes the lowest power needed for inter-cluster communication. The solution by *K. S. Manousakis and J. S. Baras* [27] first brings together the closer nodes in the network to reduce the transmission ranges. Then it assigns each node in the cluster with the lowest possible transmission range while keeping the intra-cluster connection. The pair of nodes that have the minimum distance between any two clusters are chosen as gateway nodes. The communication between the CHs is realized through these nodes. The last step is to assign the gateway nodes the lowest possible transmission range to keep the connection of the backbone network.

2.4.1.3 Optimizing route using different power level clusters

V. Kawadia and P. R. Kumar [28] group the network nodes into different power level clusters.The highest power level is needed to connect all the nodes in the entire network through multihops. A lower power level will form clusters for only the nodes that are close enough to be connected using these lower power level multihops. Each node may belong to different clusters of different power levels so that different routes are possible by taking different combinations of these power levels for each hop. Energy is then saved by optimizing these routes from source to destination

2.4.1.4 Optimizing size of k-hop cluster

The size of the cluster is important for energy saving. The small size of the cluster may result in lower total power consumption of the cluster. Yet the backbone formed by CHs of the network will become complicated. The large size of the cluster may result in a simple backbone network. Yet the transmission power in each cluster becomes higher or the mutihop route within the cluster becomes more complicated. There is then a tradeoff between the cluster size and the complexity of the backbone network. The fourth method of optimizing cluster organization therefore uses k-tree and framework in which the clustering of nodes is such that any two nodes in a cluster are at most k hops from each other. K-tree clusters are more energy efficient because the normal nodes may send data to its CH through multihops, each with lower power rather than single hop with higher power. In addition, the cluster size can be optimized by choosing the parameter k that can result in best energy saving. *S. Bandyopadhyay and E. J. Coyle* [29] proposes single-level and multi-level algorithms to cluster the nodes in the networks. In single-level algorithm, the clusters are formed in the following way: Each sensor in the network becomes a CH, called *a volunteer CH*, with probability p, and advertises itself as a CH to the sensors of no more than k hops. Any sensor that receives such advertisements and is not a CH joins the cluster. If a sensor does not receive a CH advertisement within time duration T (time needed to send data to k hops away), it can infer that it is not within k hops of any *volunteer CHs* and hence becomes *a forced CH*. In multi-level cluster algorithm, the network first elects the level-1 CHs, then level-2 CHs from the level-1 CHs. That means, the normal nodes in a higher level cluster is the CH of the lower lever cluster. The probabilities to become a CH of the node in different level clusters are $p1$, $p2$ ...ph. The hops in different level clusters are $k1$, $k2$...kh. The parameters k, T in single-level algorithm and parameters $p1$, $p2$ ...ph, $k1$, $k2$...kh in multi-level algorithm affect the power consumption of the network. Thus optimizing these parameters can reduce power consumption.

2.4.2 Averaging Power Consumption

The normal nodes in a cluster only transmit their data to their CH and will also relay the data in case of a multihop cluster. In addition to transmitting their data, the CHs also receive data from the normal nodes and relaying them. The CHs therefore consume more energy than the normal nodes, and when the CHs run out of energy the clusters break down. The power consumption of the CH will also be affected by the number of normal nodes in the cluster. Therefore energy efficiency can be improved by averaging power consumption among the nodes in the cluster through rotating the role of CH or among the CHs through assigning approximately the same number of nodes to each CH.

2.4.2.1 Rotating the role of CH in the cluster

This approach rotates the roles of CHs only within each cluster. In the re-clustering strategy and redirection scheme by *Liu and Lin* [30], periodically the node with the highest energy in the cluster is identified and re-selected as the CH, known as a redirector.

2.4.2.2 Assigning the Same Number of Nodes to Each CH

This method distributes the power consumption among CHs by assigning approximately the same number of nodes to each CH. In Base-Station Controlled Dynamic Clustering, proposed by *S. D. Muruganathan et al.* [31], the nodes are periodically reclustered by the data sink such that (1) only those nodes with higher energy levels will become CHs, (2) the CHs are uniformly spaced, and (3) the clusters have approximately the same number of normal nodes. The CH in each cluster is then randomly chosen among those higher energy level nodes [9].

2.4.3 Scheduling Active and Non-Active Nodes

There are usually many nodes within the same area in a sensor network, whereas only a smaller number of them are needed to collect the required data in that area. In the clustering scheme proposed by *Z. Abrams, et al* [32], the nodes in one area are grouped into several clusters. At a given time, we need only some of the nodes to be active while the rest are turned into energy saving state. A scheduling approach will be applied to select nodes to be active. This scheme can be applied in the high density ad hoc sensor networks.

2.5 Clustering Algorithms

2.5.1 Low-Energy Adaptive Clustering Hierarchy (LEACH):

LEACH [33] forms clusters by using a distributed algorithm, where nodes make autonomous decisions without any centralized control. Initially a node decides to be a CH with a probability p and broadcasts its decision. Each non- CH node determines its cluster by choosing the CH that can be reached using the least communication energy. The algorithm provides a balancing of energy usage by random rotation of CHs. It forms clusters based on the received signal strength and uses the CH nodes as routers to the base-station. All the data processing such as data fusion and aggregation are local to the cluster. LEACH provides the following key areas of energy savings: • No overhead is wasted making the decision of which node becomes cluster head as each node decides independent of other nodes • CDMA allows clusters to operate independently, as each cluster is assigned a different code. • Each node calculates the minimum transmission energy to communicate with its cluster head and only transmits with that power level. Changing the CH is probabilistic in LEACH; there is a good chance that a node with very low energy gets selected as a CH. When this node dies, the whole cluster becomes non functional. LEACH also forms one-hop intra- and inter cluster topology where each node can transmit directly to the CH. Then the aggregated data is transmitted to the base station. Consequently, it is not applicable to networks deployed in large regions.

2.5.2 Sensor Web or S-WEB:

S-Web [34] organizes sensors into clusters based on their geographical location without requiring the sensors to have a Global Positioning System or actively locate themselves. The S-Web enables nodes to route data packets while consuming low energy in a decentralized manner. The model is self-organizing and distributed without the need of global network knowledge. Each cluster is identified by angle order (β) and the order of Signal Strength threshold (δ). The BS in S-WEB will send beacon signals for every α degree angle, one at a time. Sensors that receive the beacons at time slot i will measure their signal strength to determine their relative distances to the BS. Let T be a predefined distance (which is inversely proportional to the received signal strength). All sensors which receive beacon signals at angle order βi ($=i*\alpha$) with signal strength of $\delta j*T$ (within sector j) will be in the same group/cluster, denoted as ($\beta i, \delta j$). Nodes with the same (β, δ) belong to the same cluster. Since nodes in the same cluster know about each other, the role of being a CH can be rotated to prolong the lifespan of CH.

2.5.3 Energy Efficient Clustering Scheme (EECS):

Energy Efficient Clustering Scheme [35] is a clustering algorithm in which cluster head candidates compete for the ability to elevate to cluster head for a given round. This competition involves candidates broadcasting their residual energy to neighboring candidates. If a given node does not find a node with more residual energy, it becomes a cluster head. Cluster formation is different than that of LEACH. LEACH forms clusters based on the minimum distance of nodes to their corresponding cluster head [10]. EECS extends this algorithm by dynamic sizing of clusters based on cluster distance from the base station. The result is an algorithm that addresses the problem that clusters at a greater range from the base station requires more energy for transmission than those that are closer. Ultimately, this improves the distribution of energy throughout the network, resulting in better resource usage and extended network lifetime. However clusters closer to the base station may become congested which may result in early CH death.

2.5.4 Hybrid Energy Efficient Distributed Clustering (HEED):

HEED [36] is a multi-hop clustering algorithm for Wireless Sensor Networks. CHs are chosen based on two important parameters: residual energy and intra-cluster communication cost. Residual energy of each node is used to probabilistically choose the initial set of CHs, as commonly done in other clustering schemes. In HEED, Intra-cluster communication cost reflects the node degree or node's proximity to the neighbor and is used by the nodes in deciding to join the cluster. Low cluster power levels promote an increase in spatial reuse while high cluster power levels are required for inter-cluster communication as they span two or more cluster areas. HEED provides a uniform CH distribution across the network and better load balancing.

2.5.5 Energy-efficient unequal clustering (EEUC):

In multi-hop WSNs, there exists a hot-spot problem that CHs closer to the base station tend to die faster, because they relay much more traffic than remote nodes. EEUC (Energy- Efficient Unequal Clustering) [37] proposed to balance the energy consumption among clusters, in which the cluster sizes near the sink node are much smaller than the clusters far away from the sink node in order to save more energy in intra-cluster communications and inter-cluster communications.

2.5.6 Power-efficient and adaptive clustering hierarchy (PEACH):

Most existing clustering protocols consume large amounts of energy, incurred by cluster formation overhead and fixed level clustering, particularly when sensor nodes are densely deployed in wireless sensor networks. To solve this problem, PEACH (Power-Efficient and Adaptive Clustering Hierarchy) [38] protocol is proposed for WSNs to minimize the energy consumption of each node, and maximize the network lifetime. In PEACH, cluster formation is performed by using overhearing characteristics of wireless communication to support adaptive multilevel clustering and avoid additional overheads.

CHAPTER 3

Problem Definition and Implementation

3.1 Problem Definition

The limited energy of sensor nodes supplied from non-rechargeable batteries is undoubtedly one of the most crucial problems in WSN. With the evolving trend in application and management of WSN, clustering provides an efficient means of managing sensor nodes in order to prolong network lifetime.

This thesis compares energy efficiency, hops and networks lifetime of the clustering algorithms, Sensor web or S-web and LEACH. S-WEB organizes sensors into clusters based on their geographical location without requiring the sensors to have a Global Positioning System or actively locate themselves. S-Web relies very little on the BS to manage the network topology and to calculate the routing paths which helps to reduce energy consumption and traffic to the BS, which can be far from the sensing field.

3.2 Implementation

There are several simulation tools available for validating the behavioral pattern of a wireless network environment such as NS-2, OPNET, OMNET++, GloMoSim, and JAVA etc. NS-2 does not provide good support for wireless sensor networks; moreover it takes long time to learn. The student version for OPNET includes support only for MANETS. OMNET++, though a good simulation tool is still new to the research community and does not have a good online support.GloMoSim lacks any online support and many source code files are deprecated for modern compilers. Therefore we have chosen JAVA as our tool for programming. The S-web and LEACH algorithms were implemented in JAVA and the simulations run for several scenarios and results analyzed. Using Java a total number of 20 nodes were randomly deployed in the area 40 X 40 m^2 field and the BS is located at the position of (0,0).Scanning angle α is 10 degree and maximum sensor distance to BS is 70 m. All nodes have the same initial energy of

0.5 Joule. We use the same radio model presented in [33], in which a radio to run the transmitter or receiver circuitry consumes E_{elec} and ε_{amp} for the transmitter amplifier. E_{elec} = $50nJ$ /bit and ε_{amp} = $100\ pJ/bit\ /m^2$.

Formulas to calculate transmitting energy E_{Tx} at a distance of d and receiving energy E_{Rx} for a k-bit packet as follows:

$E_{Tx}(k,d) = E_{elec} * k + \varepsilon_{amp} * k * d^2$ and $E_{Rx}(k) = E_{elec} * k$

A data packet here has k = 2000 bits.

We have made following assumptions concerning the network:

• All nodes are homogeneous and they have the same capabilities.

• All nodes have the same initial energy.

• The BS is placed at (0, 0), the origin of the area of deployment.

• Nodes are immobile after deployment.

• Normal nodes transmit directly to their respective cluster heads within a particular cluster

• Nodes do not have data to send all the time.

• Nodes are uniformly randomly distributed.

CHAPTER 4

Results

As discussed in previously energy is the key metric in wireless sensor networks the importance of which cannot be overemphasized. Therefore, in this section we will analyze the energy efficiency of S-web and LEACH algorithms and compare them to see how it influences the network lifetime. We consider a general communication setup where any node can communicate with any other node whether belonging to same cluster or different and the number of clusters, M=4.This sections are divided into several scenarios, energy efficiency of each scenario analyzed and corresponding network lifetimes estimated. The result shown is the average of number of hops and energy consumed. To evaluate the WSN lifespan, we simulate random sensors that have data to send and use a round as a measure unit. A round is defined as when 200 messages reach their destination.

4.1 First scenario (Normal Node to Normal Node)

In the first scenario, we consider communication between any random pair of normal nodes. We know in a clustering scheme when a normal node, that is not a cluster head, has any data to send it routes its traffic through the cluster head of the cluster to which it belongs. Also a node receives its data through its cluster head. Thus, cluster heads act as routers sending and receiving data for respective normal nodes. The following result is the average of the number of hops and consumed energy per message.

Table 1 Communication Normal Node to Normal Node

N to N	Energy (μJ)	Hops
LEACH	3812.28	6
S-Web	1932.86	3

As can be seen from the table 1, S-Web has a lower average number of hops and energy consumption per message than LEACH does. The average energy consumption for this scenario in LEACH is observed to be 3812.28 μJ whereas in case of S-Web it is 1932.86 μJ. The reason for high energy consumption in LEACH is that the cluster heads are only aware of the nodes in their own cluster. Also the BS does not have global network knowledge. Hence when a node needs to communicate to a node belonging to other cluster, its cluster head has to query the BS to know addresses of other cluster heads. Communication with BS is an energy intensive task as it is usually far away from the sensing field. This frequent communication with BS accounts for high energy consumption. However, in S-Web, the cluster heads in addition to maintaining the local cluster information also contain limited global topology information. Thus, frequent communication with BS is avoided and energy saved.

Figure 3 below illustrates network lifetime, in terms of percentage number of nodes alive against number of rounds when normal nodes randomly exchange data.

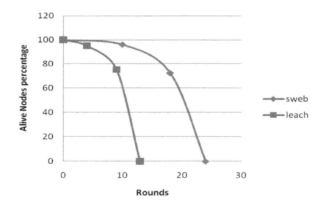

Figure 3 Network Lifetime Normal Node to Normal Node

Communication energy has a direct bearing on the time the network can operate. High energy consumption will deplete the network nodes quickly which means a shorter network lifetime.

For the given scenario, the network lifetime increases from 13 rounds in LEACH to 24 rounds when we apply the S-Web clustering mechanism.

23

4.2 Second scenario (Normal Node to Cluster Head)

In the second scenario, we consider communication between a random normal node, cluster head pair. Table 2 shows the average of the number of hops and energy consumed per message.

Table 2 Communication Normal Node to Cluster Head

N to CH	Energy (µJ)	Hops
LEACH	1937.32	3
S-Web	807.06	2

Since a cluster head itself forms the destination of data in the current scenario, it does not have to route data to any other node and hence the energy consumption is less compared to previous scenario.S-Web has a lower average number of hops and energy consumption per message than LEACH does. The average energy consumption for this scenario in LEACH is observed to be 1937.32 µJ whereas in case of S-Web it is 807.06 µJ. Owing to absence of global topology information, the cluster heads in LEACH clustering scheme require to query the BS to contact the cluster heads of other regions. On the other hand, cluster heads in S-Web also maintain limited global topology, saving the nodes from the demanding task of communication with BS.

Figure 4 shows network lifetime, in terms of percentage number of nodes alive against number of rounds.

Energy consumption has a direct impact on the time the network lifetime. Owing to lesser energy consumption, the lifetime of both the algorithms has extended, more so for S-Web. For the given scenario, the network lifetime increases from 25 rounds in LEACH to 60 rounds in S-Web.

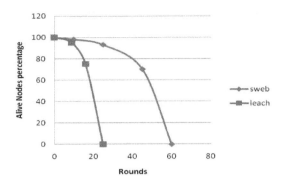

Figure 4 Network Lifetime Normal Node to Cluster Head

4.3 Third scenario (Cluster Head to Normal Node)

In this scenario, the source and destination of message have been reversed compared to second scenario. Table 3 shows the average of the number of hops and energy consumed per message.

Table 3 Communication Cluster Head to Normal Node

CH to N	Energy (μJ)	Hops
LEACH	3191.94	5
S-Web	792.23	2

For the S-Web algorithm, the current scenario is analogous to the second scenario, so energy consumption would be approximately the same (792.23 μJ and 807.06 μJ). However, in case of LEACH algorithm, when a node needs to communicate to a node belonging to other cluster, its cluster head has to query the BS to know addresses of other cluster heads. Moreover the BS itself does not contain global network topology information. This explains the high energy difference

25

for LEACH algorithm between the current scenario, 3191.94 µJ as against the second scenario 1937.32 µJ.

The network lifetime of the two algorithms for the third scenario is show in the Fig.5

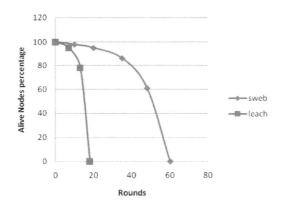

Figure 5 Network Lifetime Cluster Head to Normal Node

As the graph indicates, the lifetime of S-Web has remained largely unchanged while as for LEACH, it drops from 25 rounds (second scenario) to 18 rounds. Overall, network lifetime increases from 25 rounds in LEACH to 60 rounds in S-Web.

4.4 Fourth scenario (Cluster Head to Cluster Head)

In the fourth scenario, we consider communication between cluster heads randomly. This is the simplest among all the scenarios. Table 4 gives the average of the number of hops and energy consumption per message.

Here a cluster head itself forms both the source and destination of data. Hence, energy consumption is the minimum. The average energy consumption for this scenario in LEACH is observed to be 1312.79 µJ whereas in case of S-Web it is 422.06 µJ.

Table 4 Communication Cluster Head to Cluster Head

CH to CH	Energy (μJ)	Hops
LEACH	1312.79	2
S-Web	422.95	1

As previously discussed, the cluster heads in LEACH require to query the BS to contact the cluster heads of other regions. On the other hand, no such overhead is involved in S-Web. This accounts for lower energy in S-Web compared to LEACH.

Figure 6 is network lifetime, in terms of percentage number of nodes alive against number of rounds, for the two algorithms.

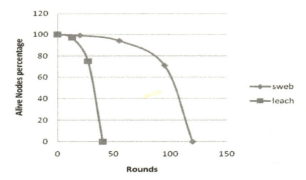

Figure 6 Network Lifetime Cluster Head to Cluster Head

Since energy consumption for this scenario is relatively small, the lifetime of both the algorithms has extended largely. For the given scenario, the network lifetime increases from 40 rounds in LEACH to 120 rounds in S-Web.

4.5 Fifth scenario (Random)

This scenario represents a high level abstraction of the previous scenarios in which communication takes place between a random pair of sensors. This scenario captures the overall trend of the network lifetime in the two algorithms. Table 5 shows the average number of hops and energy consumed per message.

Table 5 Communication between Random pairs of nodes

Random	Energy (µJ)	Hops
LEACH	2563.58	4
S-Web	988.77	2

The average energy consumption of LEACH is observed to be 2563.58µJ whereas in case of S-Web it is 988.77µJ. S-Web, thus has a lower average number of hops and energy consumption per message than LEACH. This is because sensors in S-Web can communicate with each other directly without having to go to the BS. The cluster head nodes in S-Web, in addition to the local topology information, also maintain information about the status of cluster head nodes in other clusters.

Figure 7 shows the network lifetime for communication between random pairs of sensors.

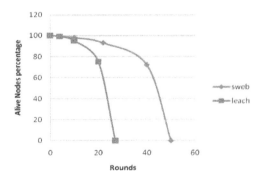

Figure 7 Network Lifetime Random pairs of nodes

As the figure clearly indicates, S-Web clustering mechanism achieves a noticeable improvement in the network lifetime. For the random scenario, the network lifetime increases from 27 rounds in LEACH to 50 rounds in S-Web. This is because sensors in S-Web can communicate with each other directly without having to go to the BS. The cluster heads in S- Web, in addition to the local topology information, also maintain information about the status of cluster heads in other clusters. This decoupling of BS from routing decisions greatly helps in improving the network lifetime.

CHAPTER 5

Conclusion and Future Work

WSN is one of the emerging and fast growing fields in the scientific world which has a wide range of applications like monitoring physical events, preparing forecasts , severe environment detection, volcano monitoring, disaster relief and battlefield surveillance.WSN are particularly helpful because they can operate unattended in harsh environments where human intervention would be inefficient, infeasible or precarious. In many applications, one wants to keep the sensor network working as long as possible. However, the network lifetime is constrained by the power supply. Researchers agree that clustering wireless sensor networks is an effective method to solve the problem of energy conservation.

In this thesis, we implement two clustering algorithms, S-Web and LEACH in JAVA and consider several scenarios to compare them on energy efficiency, number of hops and network lifetime.

The simulation results of both algorithms show that S-Web performs much better than LEACH in prolonging the lifetime of a wireless sensor network which increases from about 30 rounds in LEACH to about 50 rounds in S-Web.

As a further development, we can incorporate multihop routing to BS from farther cluster heads in S-Web algorithm, whereby cluster heads could form a multihop backbone until data reaches the BS. This could save more energy and would further prolong the WSN lifetime. Although different runs of the simulation can be considered to account for mobility of the nodes implicitly, this work can also be extended to include a well defined mobility model like the random waypoint mobility model and analyze its impact on the network lifetime. Furthermore, this work does not assume any static energy dissipation of the network nodes. This parameter can also be added to study its influence on the network life.

References

[1]   Chaurasiya, S.K.; Pal, T.; Bit, S.D., An Enhanced Energy-Efficient Protocol with Static Clustering for WSN, International Conference on Information Networking (ICOIN), 2011 Kuala Lumpur, Malaysia, on page(s): 58 – 63.

[2]   A. Abbasi, M. Younis, A survey on clustering algorithms for wireless sensor networks, Computer Communications 30 (2007) 2826-2841.

[3]   O. Boyinbode, Hanh Le, A survey on clustering algorithms for wireless sensor networks, International Conference on Network Based Information Systems IEEE computer society, 2010

[4]   Gongben Can; Shaorong Wang, A Novel Node Deployment and Clustering Scheme in Wireless Sensor Networks, Second International Symposium on Electronic Commerce and Security, 2009. ISECS '09, Nanchang, China.

[5]   Umamaheswari & G Radhamani, Clustering Schemes for Mobile Adhoc Networks : A Review, International Conference on Computer Communication and Informatics, 2012

[6]   P. Krishna, N. H. Vaidya, M. Chatterjee, and D. K. Pradhan, A cluster based approach for routing in dynamic networks, SIGCOMM Comput. Commun. Rev., vol. 27, no. 2, pp. 49– 64, 1997

[7]   S. Srivastava and R. K. Ghosh, Cluster based routing using a k tree core backbone for mobile ad hoc networks, in DIALM '02: Proceedings of the 6th international workshop on Discrete algorithms and methods for mobile computing and communications. New York, NY, USA: ACM Press, 2002, pp. 14– 23.

[8]   Y. P. Chen and A. L. Liestman, A zonal algorithm for clustering ad hoc networks. [Online]. Available: citeseer.ist.psu.edu/chen03zonal.html

[9]   D Wei, H Anthony Chan, Clustering Ad Hoc Networks: Schemes and Classifications, IEEE 2006

[10]   K. Akkaya, M. Younis, A survey on routing protocols for wireless sensor networks, Elsevier Journal of Ad Hoc Networks 3 (3) (2005) 325–349

[11]   M. Younis, M. Youssef, K. Arisha, Energy-aware management in cluster-based sensor networks, Computer Networks 43 (5) (2003) 649–668.

[12]   Y.T. Hou, Y. Shi, H.D. Sherali, On energy provisioning and relay node placement for wireless sensor networks, IEEE Transactions on Wireless Communications 4 (5) (2005) 2579–2590.

[13]   Y. Xu, J. Heidemann, D. Estrin, Geography-informed energy conservation for ad hoc routing, in: Proceedings of the 7th Annual ACM/IEEE International Conference on Mobile Computing and Networking (MobiCom'01), Rome, Italy, July 2001.

[14]   M. Adamou, I. Lee, I. Shin, An energy efficient real-time medium access control protocol for wireless ad-hoc networks, in: WIP Session of IEEE Real-time Systems Symposium (RTSS'01), London, UK, December 2001.

[15]   T. Wu, S. Biswas, A self-reorganizing slot allocation protocol for multi-cluster sensor networks, in: Proceedings of the 4th International Symposium on Information Processing in Sensor Networks (IPSN 2005), April 2005.

[16]   G. Jolly, M. Younis, An energy efficient, scalable and collision less MAC layer protocol for wireless sensor networks, Wireless Communications and Mobile Computing 5 (3) (2005) 285–304.

[17]   K. Dasgupta, K. Kalpakis, P. Namjoshi, An efficient clustering– based heuristic for data gathering and aggregation in sensor networks, in: Proceedings of the IEEE Wireless Communications and Networking Conference (WCNC, 2003), New Orleans, LA, March 2003

[18]   K. Dasgupta, M. Kukreja, K. Kalpakis, Topology-aware placement and role assignment for energy-efficient information gathering in sensor networks, in: Proceedings of 8th IEEE Symposium on Computers and Communication (ISCC'03), Kemer-Antalya, Turkey, July 2003.

[19]   I.F. Akyildiz et al., Wireless sensor networks: a survey, Computer Networks 38 (2002) 393–422

[20]   G. Gupta, M. Younis, Load-balanced clustering in wireless sensor networks, in: Proceedings of the International Conference on Communication (ICC 2003), Anchorage, Alaska, May 2003.

[21] M. Younis, K. Akkaya, A. Kunjithapatham, Optimization of task allocation in a cluster–based sensor network, in: Proceedings of the 8th IEEE Symposium on Computers and Communications (ISCC'2003), Antalya, Turkey, June 2003.

[22] E. Ilker Oyman, Cem Ersoy, Multiple sink network design problem in large scale wireless sensor networks, in: Proceedings of the IEEE International Conference on Communications (ICC 2004), Paris, June 2004.

[23] W. Heinzelman, A. Chandrakasan and H. Balakrishnan, Energy- Efficient Communication Protocol for Wireless Micro sensor Networks, Proceedings of the 33rd Hawaii International Conference on System Sciences (HICSS '00), January 2000, pp. vol.2:10.

[24] G. Gupta, M. Younis, Fault-tolerant clustering of wireless sensor networks, in: Proceedings of the IEEE Wireless Communication and Networks Conference (WCNC 2003), New Orleans, Louisiana, March 2003.

[25] W.B. Heinzelman, A.P. Chandrakasan, H. Balakrishnan, Application specific protocol architecture for wireless microsensor networks, IEEE Transactions on Wireless Networking (2002).

[26] S. Ghiasi, A. Srivastava, X. Yang, and M. Sarrafzadeh, Optimal Energy Aware Clustering in Sensor Networks, Sensors, Feb. 2002, pp. 258-269.

[27] K. S. Manousakis and J. S. Baras, Clustering for transmission range control and connectivity assurance for self configured ad hoc networks, Proc. of IEEE MILCOM 2003.

[28] V. Kawadia and P. R. Kumar, Power Control and Clustering in ad hoc Networks, Proc. of IEEE INFOCOM 2003

[29] S. Bandyopadhyay and E. J. Coyle, An energy efficient hierarchical clustering algorithm for wireless sensor Networks, Proc. of IEEE INFOCOM 2003

[30] J. S. Liu and C. H. Richard Lin, Energy-Efficiency clustering protocol in wireless sensor networks, Ad Hoc Networks, Elsevier, Volume 3, May 2005, pp371-388.

[31] S. D. Muruganathan, D. C. F. Ma, R. I. Bhasin, and A. O. Fapojuwo, A centralized energy-efficient routing protocol for wireless sensor networks, IEEE Radio Communications, March 2005, pp. S8-S13.

[32] Z. Abrams, A Goel, and S Plotkin, Set K-Cover Algorithms for Energy Efficient Monitoring in Wireless Sensor Networks, Proc. of the 3rd ACM International Symposium on Information Processing in Sensor Networks, April 2004, pp. 424-432.

[33] W. Heinzelman, A. Chandrakasan and H. Balakrishnan, Energy- Efficient Communication Protocol for Wireless Micro sensor Networks, Proceedings of the 33rd Hawaii International Conference on System Sciences (HICSS '00), January 2000, pp. vol.2:10.

[34] Le Hanh, Doan Hoang and Ravi Poliah, SWeb: an efficient and self-organizing Wireless Sensor Network Model. the 2nd International Conference on Network-Based Information Systems, Turin, Italy 2008

[35] M. Ye, C. Li, G. Chen and J. Wu, An Energy Efficient Clustering Scheme in Wireless Sensor Networks, Ad Hoc & Sensor Wireless Networks, 2006, Vol.1, pp.1–21

[36] O. Younis and S. Fahmy, HEED: A Hybrid Energy-Efficient Distributed Clustering Approach for Ad Hoc Sensor Networks, IEEE Transactions on Mobile Computing, 2004, vol. 3, no. 4

[37] C. Li, M. Ye, G. Chen, J. Wu, An energy efficient unequal clustering mechanism for wireless sensor networks, in: Proceedings of 2005 IEEE International Conference on Mobile Adhoc and Sensor Systems Conference (MASS05), Washington, D.C., pp. 604-611, November 2005.

[38] S. Yi, J. Heo, Y. Cho, and J. Hong, PEACH: power-efficient and adaptive clustering hierarchy protocol for wireless sensor networks, Computer Communications ,vol. 30, pp. 2842-2852,October

www.ingramcontent.com/pod-product-compliance
Lightning Source LLC
La Vergne TN
LVHW042305060326
832902LV00009B/1286